BRIDE'S Shortcuts and Strategies for a Beautiful Wedding

BRIDE'S Shortcuts and Strategies for a Beautiful Wedding

The Editors of *BRIDE'S* Magazine

with

Kathy C. Mullins

A Perigee Book

Perigee Books
are published by
The Putnam Publishing Group
200 Madison Avenue
New York, NY 10016

Library of Congress Cataloging-in-Publication Data
Main entry under title:

Bride's shortcuts and strategies for a beautiful wedding.

    Includes index.
    1. Weddings—United States—Planning.   2. Time
management—United States. ✓ I. Mullins, Kathy C.
II. Bride's magazine.   III. Title: Shortcuts and strategies for a
beautiful wedding.
HQ745.B82   1986   395'.22   85-25879
ISBN 0-399-51224-1

Book design by: ARLENE GOLDBERG

Printed in the United States of America

1 2 3 4 5 6 7 8 9 10

Acknowledgments

This book—like a successful wedding—was a group effort. Contributions from *BRIDE'S* editors, who are acknowledged experts in their various fields, are worthy of resounding applause. Specifically: Joyce Knoller Cohen, Maria McBride-Mellinger, and Denise O'Donoghue, who briefed us on fashion and beauty; Sally Kilbridge and Susan Farewell, who consulted with us on travel; Donna Ferrari for her expertise in entertaining; Nancy Dver, Joan Gellis-Dombrowski, and Ellie Karr, who translated our goals to retailers and wedding professionals and returned with a flood of information.

The accuracy of *BRIDE'S Shortcuts and Strategies for a Beautiful Wedding* was tried and tested from beginning to end by Andrea Feld, who lived through editing this book while planning her own wedding and whose experiences as a bride with little time to spare lend empirical authority to this timely guide. She was aided by Sharon Bonanni, whose "Etiquette Hot Line" connects us to readers' questions daily, and the entire copy staff: Laura Manske, Maribeth Maher, Susan Kuziak, and Pamela Stites, whose collective research and insights were invaluable. To Phyllis Cox, whose advice and guidance were essential; and to Yvonne Vera Spivak, who combed the files for that one perfect cover photograph.

We are equally indebted to the many recent brides and brides-to-be on *BRIDE'S* staff who shared tips, tested timetables, and helped solve problems so that you—the reader—would be spared that time-consuming activity.

And to Hedda Kleinfeld and her staff at Kleinfeld's, and Edythe Piccione and her staff at Alfred Angelo, a heartfelt "Thank you" for the time, talent, and love spent upon this worthwhile project.

Contents

Introduction

Every bride wants the luxury of planning the kind of beautiful, personal wedding she has always envisioned for herself. But every bride does not have the luxury of time. For a variety of reasons, the ideal six months-plus of planning time may be drastically shortened. Decisions may have to be made in weeks, even days rather than months. Will such haste bring negative results on your day of a lifetime? The answer emphatically is "No"! And we're here to show you why. Organizing your wedding in three months or less needn't spell hysteria. Just slow down, gather your confidence—and enjoy each moment.

It's important to remember that every wedding, even one planned in a hurry, should be a special occasion. Don't let anyone make you feel that tradition must be sacrificed in order to accelerate your timetable. This book will reassure you that like other sophisticated and knowledgeable brides today, you and your fiancé—with the help of families and friends—will be able to put together a beautiful, memorable celebration. Learn to channel your energy, now honed with anticipation and tempered by the practical skills you already possess, toward accomplishing the greatest results in the least amount of time. The bonus side effect is that developing such disciplined habits now can only be helpful later on when life means balanc-

ing the demands of marriage, children, and a career
. . . with little time to spare.

Of course, nothing will make it easier for you to
plan your wedding quickly than becoming familiar
with basic wedding etiquette. That's why I recom-
mend you take the time, right at the beginning, to
read through our *BRIDE'S Book of Etiquette.* Knowing
the accepted behavior for social rituals, such as weddings, eliminates time spent worrying about the con-
sequences of your decisions. Also, understanding the
"whys" of wedding etiquette shows you just how flexible those "rules" are, and how they'll adapt to your
own unique situation.

Here, you'll learn the "hows" of wedding planning
when every minute counts. You'll become a consum-
mate consumer, a compulsive listmaker, a resourceful
delegator. Then—with decisions made, details in
order, and plans complete—you'll be ready for a beautiful day, one that fulfills all your expectations and
that hopefully starts you both off on a life together
that includes plenty of time for each other!

Barbara Tober

Editor-in-Chief
BRIDE'S Magazine

Why Marry in a Hurry?

There's no denying that most couples today lead very busy lives. By choice or by chance, your days are filled with work, volunteer activities, appointments, classes, travel, exercise. Why, when you're so busy already, would you want to plan your wedding in such a short space of time?

Busy career couple. If your jobs have their own, sometimes pressured, demands, you two may prefer wedding planning that's least disruptive. It may seem better to tackle wedding plans in a very businesslike way, with self-imposed deadlines, even if your wedding is months away.

Job transfer. You may now be engaged or living together. If you ever thought of marrying someday, a job move may be the catalyst that makes it happen—now! Why make two moves? You two may decide to speed up the wedding plans and hire one moving van.

Illness in the family. You might choose to postpone your wedding; or, in the case of a terminal diagnosis, hasten plans to permit that person's participation.

Pregnancy. It still happens, even with careful use of birth control. To minimize any obvious developments, you may want to marry as soon as possible. Even so, there's no need these days to forfeit a joyous and traditional celebration.

Tax advantage. Just when you'd planned a spring

wedding, a promotion, stock sale, or inheritance might make a difference in your financial picture— enough to move your wedding date up before December 31st!

So in love! You're impetuous and a hopeless romantic and just can't wait. You want to get married *now.*

You may have no "reason" to hurry with your plans. But, you may still choose to adopt many of these timesaving measures. If you are sure and decisive as you move through your wedding preparations, you'll waste less time backtracking, changing your mind, repeating your steps. Plans in place, you'll have the luxury of time to anticipate all the fun ahead and, best of all, to enjoy each other!

Budgeting for Wedding Spending

Unless you're careful, shortcuts to wedding planning may increase your costs as you pay others to save you time. That's why it's important to agree on spending decisions. For some families, a wedding is a pull-out-all-the-stops occasion. The opportunity to see family and friends and to mark the joining together of two families is celebrated regally, even if money must be borrowed to make such a party possible. For other families, financial limits are essential, and that means planning and sticking to a budget.

Will both families contribute? While there is an accepted division of wedding expenses between the bride's family and the groom's, it is very common today for the groom's parents to share a greater portion of the wedding costs. But tradition still holds sway unless his family offers to do more. If so, they may choose to pay for specific items or services (band, photographer, liquor); or they may prefer to split the total figure. And, with new extended and blended households, "family" funds may come from stepmothers and stepfathers as well.

Will you two assume some of the cost? If you've both been working for a number of years, your financial position may be as comfortable as that of either set of parents. What about giving the wedding yourselves, or chipping in? Do be careful of unexpected expenditures, however, before you commit yourselves to financial obligations. If you hadn't planned on spending for hairstyling, long-distance telephone calls, taxis, honeymoon trousseau, and other beauty services, these expenses may add up to a surprising amount.

What are your borrowing resources? Your bank or a relative may be willing to lend you money to enable you to make your wedding celebration more lavish than you can afford with your present resources. But before you decide to borrow, do weigh your future financial goals—buying furniture or a car, entertaining, moving—and see if your newlywed budget can sustain the monthly payments a loan would entail.

Your Wedding Spending Worksheet

Projected wedding budget figure $_____

Contribution from bride's family   _____

Contribution from groom's family   _____

Contribution from the bride   _____

Bride's additional
  wedding-related spending   _____

Contribution from the groom   _____

Groom's additional
  wedding-related spending   _____

Borrowing:

Source of loan	Interest	Term of loan	Monthly payments

Item	Projected cost	Needed by
Rings		
Ceremony site fees		
Ceremony accessories		
candelabra		
huppah		
aisle runner		
yarmulkes		
Clergymember		
Invitations/stationery		
printing		
calligraphy		
postage		
thank-you notes		
programs		
favors		
Bridal attire		
gown		
headpiece		
shoes		
accessories		
alterations		
*Bridesmaids' attire		
gowns		
headpieces		
shoes		
accessories		
alterations		
*Groom's attire		
formalwear		
accessories		
*Ushers' attire		
formalwear		
accessories		

*Items not usually included in the bride's budget for wedding spending. Nevertheless, these expenditures must be considered in an overall spending plan, and in some cases will be assumed by the bride and/or groom.

Deposit	Source of funds	Actual cost	Amount over/under budget

Item	Projected cost	Needed by
Wedding party gifts		
*Hotel accommodations		
out-of-town guests		
wedding party		
Florist		
bridal bouquet		
bridesmaids' bouquets		
boutonnieres		
corsages		
church		
reception		
home arrangements		
Photographer		
Music		
ceremony		
reception		
Transportation		
out-of-town guests		
limousines		
getaway car		
Miscellaneous parties		
*engagement		
*office parties		
bridesmaids' luncheon		
*bachelor party		
*rehearsal dinner		
wedding breakfast		
Reception		
site		
caterer		
food		
liquor		
cake		
service		

*Items not usually included in the bride's budget for wedding spending. Nevertheless, these expenditures must be considered in an overall spending plan, and in some cases will be assumed by the bride and/or groom.

Deposit	Source of funds	Actual cost	Amount over/under budget

Item	Projected cost	Needed by
Reception (cont.)		
parking_____		
favors_____		
rentals_____		
gratuities_____		
Honeymoon		
travel_____		
accommodations_____		
meals and entertainment_____		
trousseau_____		
souvenirs_____		
photographs_____		
telegrams, flowers sent home_____		
miscellaneous extras_____		

Total projected cost $_____

Actual cost $_____

Source of extra funds   _____

Deposit	Source of funds	Actual cost	Amount over/under budget

Basic Decisions
First Things First

Few other arrangements can be made until you've settled *where* and *when* your wedding ceremony and reception will be held. You'll soon see that the two are interwoven: Your first choice of site may already be booked on the date you want. If you care about one element more than another (you *must* be married on Valentine's Day, even if the church is not available), firm up that decision first.

To help you make these decisions quickly, allow yourselves the broadest possible flexibility. Consider these issues:

Date

Do you have a wedding deadline? What are the earliest/latest possible dates?_____

Are there religious prohibitions (Lent; Rosh Hashanah)?_____

Are there dates when your clergymember is *not* available? If so, would you ask someone else?_____

_____

What are the dates your sites are available?_____

_____

What other family gatherings are scheduled in this time period? Could you combine them with your wedding?_____

Are there holiday weekends, dates of special significance (birthday, reaffirmation, or anniversary) to avoid/incorporate?_____

Expecting guests from out-of-town? If not, a weekday wedding may be easier to arrange. _____

Time

What's local custom? (In the Northeast, late afternoon is the norm for a wedding.)_____

Are there religious conventions? (Usually Jewish weddings, if held on Saturday, the Sabbath, begin no sooner than one hour after sundown.)_____

Consider your families and other special guests. What time of day would be most convenient for travel plans?_____

What's the degree of formality of your wedding? It usually dictates an appropriate hour (very formal attire is usually worn at high noon, late afternoon, or evening). _____

Will you serve light refreshments only, a full meal? At what time of day would that menu be suitable?___

Should climate be considered? (In hot weather, evening weddings may be more comfortable.)_____

Site

Should the ceremony site be religious? Do you have a church/synagogue affiliation?_____

What is the approximate size of your guest list?_____

Would you consider having the ceremony/reception in the same place? At home? Outdoors?_____

Are you looking for an unusual site? Would you consider an arboretum, cruise ship, castle, inn, nightclub, college campus, historical site, museum, sports facility, studio, restaurant?_____

What characteristics, equipment should your ideal site have?_____

How many hours do you wish to reserve for the reception?_____

Choices

	1st	2nd	3rd
Ceremony			
date_____			
time_____			
site_____			
Reception			
time_____			
site_____			

Setting Wedding Style Priorities

Gather Necessary Information

Hone your investigative skills. To get the maximum benefit, you need to compare costs and services. Do write down all your questions before you visit a store or place a telephone call so you get all the facts you need on the first go-round. Some examples:

· Who? What's the name and phone number of the vendor, so confirmations, questions can be addressed directly; how reliable are any sub-contractors used by this vendor?

· What? Exactly what will the vendor offer you, do for you?

· Why? Is this wedding service/item necessary or merely customary; are there other options?

· When? Can services be rendered in time; could this event be postponed until after the ceremony; when must your order be placed to meet the time-table?

· Where? Is the vendor limited to one location to perform a service? Will he travel to your location? Transport equipment?

· How much? What will it cost; when is money needed; what could reduce/escalate the price?

· What if? Is there a second choice in case something goes wrong; what circumstances might alter the plans; can you get a written guarantee?

Network with colleagues and friends. Find out about reception sites, honeymoon possibilities by putting out feelers to friends and business associates. Read articles, visit wedding professionals (florists, bakers, musicians) for specific information and referrals. Talk to national trade associations too (e.g., the Professional Photographers of America, Inc. in Des Plaines, Illinois) if you can't get questions answered locally.

Decide on Personal Preferences

Your heads will soon be whirling with options. In order to create your own wedding plan, you and your fiancé have some decisions to make. What's the best way of tackling them?

Brainstorm with family and friends. Pore over bridal magazines, cut out pictures of styles that appeal, talk about family, cultural, and religious traditions.

Discuss feelings with each other. Be honest about things that are important, or suggestions that make you uncomfortable. State your favorites; how else will anyone know what they are?

Make compromises you can live with. A wedding involves two people. You probably won't agree on every aspect of your plans, yet each of you should be pleased—and excited—with the results.

Your Wedding Calendar Worksheets

Three-Month Plan

12 WEEKS BEFORE:

Buy bridal magazines, etiquette book, wedding planner. Get a feel for your wedding tastes.

Discuss future lifestyle with your fiancé. Begin selecting colors, china, silver, furnishings favorites.

Visit Wedding Gift Registry. Fill out preference sheets.

Decide on and set up gift recording system.

Hold engagement party.

Discuss wedding budget with your fiancé and family. If your fiancé's family offers to share expenses, include them in the talks. Decide on wedding style, where you'll splurge, cut corners. Establish firm spending limits.

Choose wedding and reception sites. Make reservations.

Visit clergymember or judge with fiancé. Set date and time for wedding rehearsal. Arrange appointments for further planning, premarital couple counseling.

Hire a reception band. Begin assembling a list of musical favorites.

Decide on size of wedding party. Invite attendants to participate.

Shop for your dress, accessories. Order them now.

Select engagement and wedding rings. Order engraving.

Determine the number of guests your sites and budget can accommodate.

Tell each family to begin drawing up guest list.

Talk about honeymoon preferences. Visit travel agents for ideas.

Inquire about transportation rentals in your area. Evaluate needs for wedding day, out-of-towners' transport.

Make an appointment with gynecologist. Decide on birth-control method, or reevaluate current method.

10 WEEKS BEFORE:

Order invitations, announcements, thank-you note paper, imprinted favors. Insist on proofreading copy.

Complete your guest list. Devise file system to keep track of replies.

Plan color scheme for wedding, reception.

Shop with attendants for dresses. Order, make appointments for fittings. Help your mothers decide on colors, styles for their dresses.

Confirm delivery date for your dress. Schedule first fitting.

Select portrait photographer. Set date of sitting when delivery of your dress is assured.

Inquire about newspaper publicity guidelines.

Select men's formalwear. Decide how to obtain ushers' measurements.

Make final decision about honeymoon destination. Book all reservations. Traveling abroad? Obtain or update passport, get necessary shots.

Select wedding planning volunteers; decide how to divvy up jobs.

Get hair cut and styled; have facial and manicure; exercise and watch diet.

8 WEEKS BEFORE:

Get estimates, select photographer, videographer. Begin listing "can't miss" shots.

Consult with florist. Bring fabric swatches, select floral scheme.

Choose caterer and decide on menu. Plan table decorations, reception space. Order wedding cake.

Meet with clergy to plan ceremony—vows, readings, music, program booklets, ethnic traditions.

Go over ceremony needs, details with church secretary, sexton, organist.

Pick up invitation envelopes. Begin addressing them.

6 WEEKS BEFORE:

Reserve all transportation—limousine, carriage, jitney—to pick up, deliver, guests.

Arrange for all rentals. Hire service personnel.

Reserve blocks of lodging for out-of-town guests, your wedding party.

4 WEEKS BEFORE:

Buy wedding gifts for each other.

Mail invitations. Choose a pretty stamp and be sure to use correct postage!

Have final dress, headpiece fittings. Wear the undergarments and shoes you will use on the wedding day.

Choose gifts for attendants.

Have formal portrait taken.

Submit publicity information to newspapers.

Plan bridesmaids' luncheon.

Make plans for rehearsal dinner.

Write thank-you notes as gifts are received.

Purchase additional luggage, do final trousseau shopping.

Check on legalities. Get blood tests, obtain marriage license. If changing your name, revise official documents.

2 WEEKS BEFORE:

Arrange for gift protection on the wedding day; purchase "floater" on insurance policy or hire a security guard.

Schedule hair and manicure appointments for the wedding day.

Design seating charts for reception. Begin lettering place cards.

Prepare toasts for rehearsal dinner, reception.

Confirm honeymoon reservations. Pick up airline tickets.

Hold bridesmaids' luncheon, bachelor party.

1 WEEK BEFORE:

Arrange for guest parking, contingency plans for traffic problems.

Remind wedding attendants about rehearsal time, duties, schedules. Verify their accomodations and arrival times.

Make list of last-minute details (e.g., gratuities, gifts).

Mentally visualize each aspect of your wedding. Look for omissions: Do you have a cake knife? Who will say the blessing over dinner? Are attendants' gifts wrapped? Where will you touch up your makeup, change your clothes?

Take time for a massage, nightly relaxing baths.

Pack for honeymoon. Arrange for your departure transportation, traveler's checks, extras (a bottle of champagne).

Prepare announcements for mailing immediately after ceremony.

Give caterer the final guest count.

Arrange to pick up formalwear.

Confirm all deliveries and arrangements.

Attend rehearsal, rehearsal dinner.

Eight-Week Plan

8 WEEKS BEFORE:

Scout out wedding ideas by looking at bridal books, magazines, talking to friends.

Meet with families. Set wedding style, budget, size. Make a tentative timetable for the eight weeks. How can each person help? What professionals should be hired? Make a list of needed information, delegate research tasks.

Visit officiant to discuss ceremony date, time, options.

If you are hiring a wedding consultant, do it now.

Compare reception sites for availability, cost. Think about having your party at your home.

Set firm date, time, place for wedding. Notify families. Begin compiling guest lists.

7 WEEKS BEFORE:

Reserve ceremony and reception sites.

Compare estimates and services of photographers, musicians, bakers, caterers, florists, stationers.

Shop for bridal gown. Be sure delivery can be assured by the week before the wedding. Take time to select accessories. Schedule fittings.

Choose wedding color scheme. Shop for bridesmaids' and mothers' dresses. Ask for fabric swatch to match with shoes, bouquets.

Order invitations. Be sure to proofread before printing begins. Purchase thank-you note paper at the same time. Ask for envelopes ahead of invitations so you may start addressing.

6 WEEKS BEFORE:

Meet with officiant to plan the ceremony. List every decision to be made—hymns, readings, scripture, programs—and the deadline for each decision. Make appointments for future meetings, couple counseling. Schedule the rehearsal.

Register your preferences at the Wedding Gift Registry.

Begin a beauty regime that includes hairstyling, manicure, skin care, exercise, and healthy eating habits.

Call newspapers about publicity. Determine if there is time to arrange for photograph. Make all arrangements.

Select rings. Is there time for engraving?

Make decisions about the reception—what's the setup, agenda, menu?

Discuss honeymoon preferences with your fiancé. Go away now or later? For how long? Where?

Hire all wedding professionals. Get *specific* contracts.

Complete guest list.

5 WEEKS BEFORE:

Address invitation envelopes.

Choose, order formalwear. Call each usher for exact sizes.

Begin couple counseling.

Plan music for ceremony and reception with organist and band leader.

Set up file system for gifts, guest replies.

Go for first dress fitting. Be sure to take all accessories—undergarments, shoes, headpiece.

Choose all floral arrangements when your color scheme is set. Think about all your flower needs at once—corsages, boutonnieres, table decorations, thank-you gifts, pew markers, welcome baskets in guest rooms.

Select cake flavors, frosting, decoration, cake topper.

4 WEEKS BEFORE:

Mail invitations.

Reserve rooms for out-of-town guests.

Check with banquet manager or caterer. Anything missing? See that every reception need is on order—rentals, service personnel, favors, liquor, sound system, candles, hors d'oeuvres.

Visit photographer. Decide on amount of film, whether black and white or color; discuss type of shots.

Book honeymoon travel, accommodations.

Plan rehearsal dinner.

Check with civil authorities about legal requirements.

Visit doctor for blood tests, birth-control advice.

3 WEEKS BEFORE:

Start writing thank-you notes. Keep up as gifts arrive.

Shop for your trousseau, party clothes, wedding gifts to each other, attendants' gifts.

Arrange for all transportation; also, parking space, traffic problems.

Make moving plans. Decide how, when. Get estimate on mover or van rental. Reserve time with mover.

Plan bridesmaids' luncheon. Wrap gifts.

Let friends know when a shower might be fun.

2 WEEKS BEFORE:

Go with fiancé to get marriage license. Celebrate this special occasion.

Make a list of important people at the reception, shots you want the photographer to catch. Be sure to include a timetable of scheduled events so photographer can be in the right spot when needed.

Write out a day-of-the-wedding checklist. Ask a trusted friend to be in charge.

Think through ceremony, reception movements. Attend to omissions; who will pass the guest book, stand in the receiving line, drive the bridal car, etc.?

Have final dress fitting.

Call all non-respondents; call caterer with final guest count.

1 WEEK BEFORE:

Have portrait taken for wedding keepsake if not done earlier.

Set up gift display, invite friends to view it. Don't forget security and insurance.

Draw up a seating plan. Letter place cards.

Attend bachelor, bridesmaids' parties.

Move some belongings to new home or confirm post-wedding moving date.

Pack for honeymoon or weekend trip.

Confirm all arrangements, deliveries. Itemize specifics when you call.

Attend rehearsal, rehearsal dinner.

WEDDING DAY:

Enjoy time with your family.

Prepare with hair appointment, manicure, makeup session, or do these yourself.

Thirty-Day Plan

Day 1: Organize the next month's work calendar to arrange for several days off now and at wedding time. Your fiancé should do the same. Read bridal magazines and books and talk with each other about wedding style priorities, budget, basic decisions. Make an appointment with your officiant.

Day 2: Meet with families. Discuss your preferences, theirs. Set style, finances, size of wedding. Do you need to hire a wedding consultant or secretarial service? Jot down suggestions for sites.

Day 3: Decide on date, time, and site of the wedding. Telephone sites, visit only good prospects. Meet with officiant. Reserve ceremony and reception sites. Invite attendants to participate in wedding.

Day 4: Order invitations—rush! If you cannot get a 48-hour printing service, organize a telephone brigade to alert guests to save the date. Order other printing needs; announcements are not a rush. List things to do. Delegate jobs to family members, friends.

Day 5: Shop for your gown, accessories. If a special order, get firm delivery date, schedule fitting.

Day 6: Register for gift choices at your favorite department store, specialty shop. Select one with computer registry but be sure you can get "on line" quickly.

Day 7: Check newspaper publicity requirements. If there's time, get forms, fill out, submit to Society Editor. There's probably not time to complete wedding outfit and sit for a publicity portrait, so see if an announcement can run afterward using a wedding-day photograph.

Day 8: Issue invitations. Assemble a team to address, stamp, mail, envelopes.

Day 9: Shop for bridal attendants' gowns and accessories. Set fitting date.

Day 10: Select band, photographer, florist, caterer, videographer.

Day 11: Visit formalwear store. Choose style, reserve sizes. Ask for measurement cards, then telephone each usher for correct measurements—especially length.

Day 12: Talk with your groom-to-be about wedding night, weekend, or honeymoon plans. Will you honeymoon now or later? If you opt for later, reserve a hotel or country inn for a luxurious weekend respite after the wedding. Or, book honeymoon trip.

Day 13: Choose reception menu with caterer. Take fabric swatches to florist, make selections.

Day 14: Meet with officiant, go over ceremony details. Plan service, including all personal touches. Begin couple counseling, then schedule future sessions. Select ceremony music with organist, other musicians.

Day 15: Meet with banquet manager or caterer to choose tablecloths, table decorations. Arrange for rentals, discuss use of space. Plan menu, mention special dietary needs. Order wedding cake.

Day 16: Visit gynecologist for checkup, birth-control consultation. Get blood tests taken.

Day 17: Shop for wedding bands or ask family about antique or heirloom rings.

Day 18: Arrange all transportation for arrivals and departures, ceremony, honeymoon, or weekend trip.

Day 19: Purchase reception guest book. If by telephone—rush. Plan rehearsal dinner.

Day 20: Go together to obtain marriage license. Take time out to have dinner, relax.

Day 21: Have hair styled.

Day 22: Begin thank-you notes, just one a day if time is short. Shop for gifts—attendants, family thank-yous.

Day 23: Deliver sheet music, song list to reception musicians.

Day 24: Write out list of photo "musts."

Day 25: Have final dress fitting.

Day 26: Invite attendants to a post-wedding bridesmaids' party with hand-written notes that say "thank-you" now, but indicate a more personal expression of gratitude will follow.

Day 27: Design reception seating chart, write out place cards.

Day 28: Confirm all arrangements; answer any last-minute questions with florist, caterer, band, photographer, musicians. Give caterer final guest count.

Day 29: Go over final details. Attend rehearsal, rehearsal dinner.

Day 30: Have hair done, nails manicured. Arrive at ceremony calm, poised, and ready to have a terrific time.

Post-Wedding Schedule for the Thirty-Day Plan

1ST WEEK:
Wedding trip or weekend—relax and enjoy.

Shop for wedding party gifts and mementos.

Keep an eye out for a wedding gift for your groom. It will be a memento of your trip too.

Arrange for announcement in local, professional, college newspapers.

2ND WEEK:
Address wedding announcements, mail.

Confirm moving plans with professionals or friends.

Move any furniture, clothing, household goods, wedding presents to new home.

Continue thank-you notes. (If you did not have time for wedding favors, you might order photo thank-yous.)

3RD WEEK:
Belated bachelor party and bridesmaids' luncheon or dinner—a nice time to give attendants gifts.

If changing your name, update legal documents.

4TH WEEK:
Redo wedding-day hairstyle and makeup, have formal portrait taken. Check wedding gown for any spots

that would show in photo.

Friends might host a co-ed post-wedding shower with a his-and-hers gift theme.

Finish all thank-you notes.

2 MONTHS:

If you put off selecting or designing a special engagement or marriage ring, begin shopping for ring, stone, designer. Do you want it completed for first anniversary, honeymoon trip?

Was honeymoon trip postponed? Talk about your trip now. Make arrangements with travel agent. Shop for trousseau, luggage. Arrange for passports, shots, travel needs.

3–6 MONTHS:

Take your long-awaited honeymoon trip. Shower yourselves with wedding memories beforehand—view slides or videotapes, look at your photograph albums, sip champagne.

Schedule Your Time Priorities

You'll need to turn your ideas and style preferences into step-by-step plans that make the wedding you've envisioned a reality.

Arrange tasks in "domino" sequence. As you review your ideas, you'll see that certain arrangements must be completed before others can be started. For instance, you must confirm reservations with the church and reception hall before you can print invitations; choose bridesmaids' colors prior to selecting your floral scheme.

Do what's most important first. If you care more about menu than flowers, give the reception fare your early and complete attention. Then, tend to floral decorations.

Give each item a priority rating. With these in mind, begin making lists, setting deadlines, delegating chores—in order of importance:

- TOP PRIORITY (those arrangements that are pivotal to the main event, such as reserving the church, synagogue, or reception hall).

- VERY IMPORTANT (things that are essential and require time for selection and preparation, such as selecting the invitations, shopping for your gown).

- AS SOON AS POSSIBLE (those decisions that can be made in less time, such as choice of music, selecting readings).

- IF TIME ALLOWS (ideas that would be nice to include, but may have to be dropped if time runs out, such as homemade favors, calligraphic place cards, wedding programs).

- LAST-MINUTE BY NECESSITY (jobs with no time flexibility, such as getting blood tests, applying for the marriage license, final dress fittings).

Tips for Time Management

If you are planning a wedding in less than six months, you have no time to waste. Use these tips to help organize yourself.

Make an overall game plan. Visualize your wedding day. Like a jigsaw puzzle, your vision will become more visible as each completed arrangement fits into place.

Set priorities that work for you. Otherwise, you'll resist pursuing those goals.

Know yourself and your task. Choose the most productive times to tackle jobs: Don't go shopping during your daily "slump" time; visit stores when least crowded so you can get service, answers; don't run across town at rush hour—choose a more practical time to complete that errand.

Write out lists and update them each day: "Things to Do Today"; "Things to Do Next."

Assess resources, then delegate. Give clear directives; followup; mark progress.

Use deadlines to get things done. Otherwise, Parkinson's Law applies: "Work expands to fill the time available for its completion."

Take notes. Write down estimates, impressions, names. If you rely on memory alone, you'll end up retracing your steps.

Curtail interruptions. Keeping your families and the

wedding party informed is more efficient than stopping to answer questions. How? By a "progress" report. Return telephone calls in bunches—you'll spend less time at it.

Take advantage of unexpected free time to accomplish something. Write thank-yous while waiting for an appointment; update lists while riding the bus.

Fight procrastination. Do tasks you're avoiding first, so you don't get bogged down; divide overwhelming tasks into several manageable jobs.

Seek excellence rather than perfection. Because it's never possible to achieve, perfection is a paralyzer.

Five Tips for Keeping Track While on the Fast Track

1. Have a place for everything; take time to put everything in its place. Then you won't waste time searching for telephone numbers, clippings, contracts. Use a card file or source notebook.
2. Carry your planner with you. A separate briefcase or folder with wedding planning information, notebook, is very compact and portable. Just grab it when you switch gears from workplace to wedding tasks.
3. Organize a system for recording R.S.V.P. replies, gifts as they arrive. Note gift donor, complete gift description, store, date of arrival, and date you send thank-you note.
4. Work with a list; update frequently.
5. Chart your traffic patterns so you can accomplish several tasks in one trip.

Divide-and-Conquer Tasks

A wedding is not a one-woman show. A rush wedding, more than any other, can only be accomplished with teamwork. The team may be just you and your groom. It may be the two of you and both families. Or, it may include a large circle of friends.

Effective Teamwork

Learn these principles of teamwork to make your managerial job easier:

· Someone must always be in charge—and that's probably you!

· Communication keeps things moving along.

· Team members must think their work is important and that nonperformance will be noticed. Set deadlines.

· Thank-yous and praise go a long way.

· Know when to step in and do it yourself.

Organizing Your Help

Delegating tasks takes some extra planning in the beginning but it ensures that lots can be accomplished in a short time. It can be fun too! Your helpers can take on a variety of jobs:

Wedding work parties—
Spruce up the yard for at-home reception.
Collate and staple programs.
Address wedding invitations.
Move belongings to new home.
Shopping legwork—
Scout accessories.
Shop for bridesmaids' dresses.
Preview headpieces, bouquets.
Food preparation—
Prepare identical main dishes from your recipes.
Shop for supplies.
Find rental source for large platters and bowls.
Fix favorite hors d'oeuvres.
Transportation—
Mobilize airport pick-up service for out-of-town guests.
Run last-minute errands.
Taxi guests from hotels to activities.
Emergencies—
Serve as troubleshooter for crises.

Everyone Gets in Step

Not only will your wedding team have to speed up their regular prewedding duties, each may have to assume a heavier load in order to get everything done on time! How might each role expand? In some instances, you'll need to assess talents, availability, and location before you ask for help. Then, don't be vague; say exactly what you need each person to do.

Groom. If there are only thirty planning days, your fiancé should also take time off from work at the very beginning so your most basic plans can be put in place quickly. Since organizing a wedding is not something one does frequently, both of you can learn as you go. Just divide up the major planning areas and ask for help—or another opinion—when you falter. Your groom-to-be could take charge of the music and flowers while you see to the menu and invitations. Check decisions with each other.

Bridesmaids. A nearby woman friend can be helpful with local chores, such as taking shoes to be dyed. But even a faraway bridesmaid can help. Your college friend might research readings and music at the school library. Again, a specific request ("We both love e.e. cummings; would you look for an appropriate poem for our ceremony?") gets better results than just asking people to "think up some ceremony ideas."

Mothers. Try to make every request lead to useful results. If you're including reception traditions from your fiancé's Hungarian background, ask his mother for actual recipes, not just menu ideas. She may then offer to ask family members to bake the specialties. If not, the recipes can be passed along to your caterer. A mother who loves to shop might scour stores for imaginative bridesmaids' gifts, and come back with prices, even order numbers. A seasoned party-giver could plan the menu, table decor, and centerpieces.

Fathers. They're an underutilized resource. Yours might arrange for the invitation printing, coordinate the guest list, and order the liquor. Your fiancé's father might take care of transportation, parking, or out-of-town guest reservations.

Ushers. An experienced groomsman could help by typing up job descriptions for the other men in the wedding party. Another could draw up a reception dance-tune list. A friend could save you time by rounding up the legal forms needed for changing your name on bank accounts, driver's license, stock certificates—and deliver them when completed.

Gathering Information

Every wedding professional will be able to help you find at least one shortcut. Remember to ask! And be prepared for your first meeting or telephone call so you'll be able to set wheels in motion immediately.

Religious Considerations

When you meet with your officiant, you'll save time if you've discussed these questions ahead of time with your fiancé:

- Why is a religious ceremony important?
- Will the service be in a sanctuary, your home, outdoors?
- Will you personalize the standard ceremony?
- Will it be an interfaith service?
- What do you want to say about a previous marriage?
- Where are your divorce papers?
- How much time can you allow for prenuptial counseling?

Remember that counseling may slow you down. Your clergymember may require premarital counseling over a span of time—ten weeks or three months. Some Roman Catholic dioceses are advocating a six-month wait to allow better preparation for marriage. If confronted with that requirement, you may have to suggest to the clergymember ways of honoring that intent in a shorter time. Couples contemplating marriage might attend couple group sessions, lectures, meetings with the clergymember or a marriage counselor, Engaged Encounter weekends.

Divorce and interfaith marriage can also cause delays. In both civil and religious law there are necessary steps to undo a previous marriage. You cannot remarry in a house of worship unless you meet these requirements. If divorced, say so during your first conversation with the clergymember and find out what's required. As for interfaith weddings, you may encounter more or less difficulty arranging your ceremony, depending on your faith. It may require paperwork; it definitely will involve the approval of the host clergymember. Indicate that religion is important to each of you. If you meet resistance to the idea of interfaith marriage, it's probably the cleric's personal belief rather than a doctrinal position. Try another clergymember.

Finally, consider scheduling. Each church or temple has services and events that may stand in the way of your ideal timetable; for instance, your preferred date may be a Holy Day when weddings are not performed.

When you meet with the officiant, you will need to ask about:

· *equipment* available from the church or temple—aisle carpet, huppah, pew tapers, kneeler;

· *fees* of clergymember, organist, sexton;

· *regulations* concerning photography, type of music, decoration of the santuary, use of liquor on premises, seating capacity of church or temple, throwing of rice or rose petals;

· *length of the ceremony* and how much time you can count on for setting up, clearing the building;

· *wording of the ceremony.* (Request a copy of the standard wedding text at this time too.)

Wedding Gift Registry

Your Wedding Gift Registry will help you organize your gift preferences quickly and efficiently. Many are computerized for easy up-dates and long-distance use. Here, some questions you may have.

How can a Wedding Gift Registry help me? Its consultant can give advice to focus your thinking about gift choices. (Consider your groom's preferences as well as your own and choose styles and colors together.) It will keep track of gifts purchased. It will also solve problems and let guests know where to send the gifts if you're moving, marrying in another town (shipment to a new address, or your parents' home). The consultant can answer questions about how to encourage large chip-in gifts or handle returns and exchanges. Finally, the Registry will offer convenient listings at branch stores. The computer has made it possible to help guests across the country choose the right gift for you.

Where should I register? At a large department store you'll continue to use; perhaps specialty stores, such as a wine and spirits emporium, sports shop, bookstore, kitchenware boutique, or even a museum. But before you choose, ask: Is there stock so guests can obtain gifts quickly? What's the return policy? Are there services such as gift wrapping and delivery? Does the store have branches in other cities? Are the sales personnel courteous and helpful? Is there a wide price range of gift choices?

How do I register? First you must make an appointment. You'll want someone's immediate and undivided attention. State your wedding date and ask if this store can work within your timetable. Can they rush you "on line" for computer registry? *Ask.* Go prepared with some ideas about preferences, entertaining style, favorite colors, larger gifts. Take a standardized registry form and fill it in while walking around the store together. Finally, do plan to spend enough time at the store to complete your selections.

List all categories—and don't forget hobby accessories, sports equipment, lawn and garden tools, books.

Bridal Shows

If you're really at sea about your personal wedding style and overwhelmed with the idea of running around to many different displays, a bridal show, with multiple ideas and services gathered in one place, will really save you time. Look for a show in your area—but you'll have to be lucky in your timing, since these are usually scheduled to coincide with peak sales periods.

A show might be sponsored by a department store (often in conjunction with a bridal magazine), or a service company at a shopping mall. The store show is geared to merchandise it sells, while the showcase sponsored by a service company will give you an overview of styles and services available in your area. You'll come away with sources for florists, videographers, home furnishings, music management, formalwear, and more. You and your fiancé should go together and talk about your choices. It saves you shopping time and helps you focus—together. Check newspaper advertisements, radio spot announcements, store promotions, or ask the store consultant at the Wedding Gift Registry to keep you posted about upcoming shows.

Mail-order Shopping

If you do not live near a large shopping center (and even if you do), it may be faster and more convenient to shop for some wedding products by mail. You may be surprised at the array—bridal fabric, lace, toasting glasses, invitations, wedding accessories, gifts, pantyhose—available by mail. Where to find the companies that offer these items? Bridal magazines and newspaper wedding supplements are excellent sources. Obtain catalogs right away. Telephone your order (there may be a toll-free number); it's faster than writing, and say you'll pay for Express Mail delivery. Be sure to deal with reputable companies (check with friends and the Better Business Bureau). Finally, remember that it's unwise to rely on mail order during holiday periods.

Consumer Know-how

Buyer beware! This advice is never more important than when you are in a hurry, and haste may mean wasting your valuable time correcting mistakes.

Don't say, "It's a rush," or the price may go up needlessly. Once you've been quoted a price and a time frame, you may have to pay extra for special handling.

Mistakes are costly as well as time-consuming: double-check; proofread; confirm everything; get second opinions.

What you see may not be what you get. Be specific, ask questions, take down names.

Ask for references. A reputable firm, proud of its record, will be glad to oblige with names of previous customers.

Contracts are important forms of self-protection. You should sign one for every service you order, including the florist, photographer, caterer, banquet manager, musicians, baker, and limousine company. A stationer may have a blank form that you could adapt to your needs, or draw up a letter of your own. A service contract should always stipulate the date of service, time of delivery, price, hours of service, and terms of cancellation. In addition, keep these details in mind:

Contract with photographer: Specify name of the person taking pictures; number of rolls of film; who keeps proofs, negatives; expected attire for photographer; what's included in any package deal; delivery date for proofs; whether total cost includes an album; compensation for poor-quality photographs.

Contract with musicians: Specify name of the group leader; the names and instruments of musicians; name of singer; amount of playing time, break time; total cost; overtime or extra charges.

Contract with florist: Specify names of flowers to be used; type of arrangement or bouquet and number of each; hours for setup; live or artificial flowers; colors to be used; total cost.

Contract with caterer: Specify names and size of dishes, specific cuts or brands; number of service people; hours of reception, meal, service; number of guests to be served; disposition of uneaten food; colors, table decorations; amounts and brands of liquor; flavors, size, decoration of wedding cake; order and schedule of service; policy for "no-shows"; deadline for final guest count; number of special menu meals and cost; name of maître d'hôtel and duties; total cost; overtime or extra charges.

Legalities

Chances are, there will be rules attached to all the paperwork required to make your wedding "official." The rules may be determined by the state (age you may marry without consent), city (hours the municipal office will allow you to apply for a marriage license), or a religious organization (length of time following a divorce that a church marriage may take place).

There are also rules connected with your specific house of worship. Since you don't have time to tilt at windmills, work within the limits or choose another place to marry.

Marriage license. Each state sets its own regulations. Age, rules for blood test and waiting period are variables. A marriage is not legal without a valid license, so call your wedding site municipality for requirements and obtain required forms.

Marriage contract. Your marriage is a legal contract, whose wording is stipulated by your state unless you two agree to modify it with another contract. Yours might stipulate ownership of property, your understanding of marriage roles, the inheritance rights of children from a previous marriage. Such a contract is entirely optional, but if you intend to have one, find time to have a lawyer draw it up before the wedding.

Blood test. Not every state requires a blood test, but where used, its purpose is to screen for sexually transmitted diseases, particularly venereal disease. Check with your wedding locality to see if you should schedule a doctor's visit.

Religious requirements. You may be asked to sign an agreement to marry according to religious laws. And, if one of you is divorced or of another faith, there may be additional paperwork. A fixed amount of counseling may be mandated. Though the religious denomination or organization sets standards for regulations, individual clergy may vary in flexibility about meeting obligations. Try another church or synagogue before you turn to a civil wedding.

Changing your name. It's not required. A married woman may keep her own surname, but she must then use it consistently. If you do take your husband's name, record that change on all legal documents and important papers.

Financial arrangements. There's no obligation to change over bank accounts or stocks or write a will before your wedding, but it's wise to take care of these matters as quickly as possible.

Passport. Honeymooning in a foreign country? Most likely, you'll need a passport. Apply in person at any county clerk's office, authorized post office, or federal passport agency. Bring proof of your identity, citizenship. A passport may not be obtained in your married name before you are actually married, so plan to use your maiden name. You may find that taking along a photocopy of your marriage certificate saves you trouble in those countries that might question your marital status.

Planning Tools and Resources

Bridal Magazines

You'll find the latest issues on the newsstand a treasure chest of information. Since you won't have time to wait for the publication of future issues, read back issues instead at your local library for wedding planning tips. Back issues offer one other advantage: Fashions previewed in them may now be seen in the stores, and are more readily available from the manufacturers, with production snags all worked out—a boon when your wedding date is just around the corner.

The Telephone

When you're in need of quick information, "Let your fingers do the walking" is good advice. You can locate a shop that carries the bridal gown you admired, call florists to learn what blooms are in season, or order wedding accessories. Too expensive for your budget? Not available when you need it? Your telephone calls will eliminate those nonproductive visits or shopping excursions. And toll-free telephone numbers save you money as well as time. A call to the telephone company's toll-free information service (1-800-555-1212), with the exact name of the company or association you're trying to reach, will provide you with the toll-free number, if one exists.

The Library

A trip to the library can save you (or your researcher) time and legwork by locating books on wedding etiquette or customs, recordings of wedding music, magazine articles on wedding planning, travel guides for honeymoon spots, all under one roof. Your librarian can help you locate sources for more specific needs, such as: cake recipes or decorating tips; ethnic wedding traditions; quotations or inspirational passages for ceremony readings; college music collections.

The Computer

If you already know how to use a computer (and this isn't the time to learn!), you'll find it very helpful now. A computer can be your central information bank, filing data such as names, addresses, telephone numbers of guests and vendors; collecting facts about who's accepted invitations, received a thank-you note, signed a contract. You can use your computer to keep track of wedding spending and list things to do each day, or even design your seating plan.

Personal Notebook or Tape Recorder

Carry a notebook in your purse or briefcase for on-the-spot note taking. Or, if you'd rather, speak your thoughts into a portable tape recorder. Jot down prices, colors, strong impressions about sites. Turn it on when you're "interviewing" a band. Got a bright idea? Get it down on paper or tape before you forget.

Rental Companies

Furnish your reception party space quickly with equipment, both standard (china, chafing dishes, flatware) and exotic (jukebox, special effects lighting, video playback machines). Check out shops that lease furniture, props, costumes, and decorative objects.

Ten Planning Shortcuts

When Money Is No Object

1. Hire a wedding consultant.
2. Be willing to pay for express service and delivery, once you've been quoted regular prices and delivery times. Everything from printing to portrait finishing can be hurried—for a price.
3. Transfer the entire task of addressing invitations to a calligrapher or social secretary. It's attractive and out of your hands entirely. Just be sure your list is very specific, with titles written out exactly as you want them to appear on inner and outer envelopes. Do order extra envelopes in case of mistakes.
4. Have your reception in a full-service facility so that many details (parking, tending bar) will be looked after by their staff.
5. Set up your own beauty salon in your home or hotel room on the wedding day. Have a hairstylist, manicurist, makeup artist, and masseuse on hand to pamper you, your mothers, your attendants.
6. Establish an acount with a car or limousine service; or, hire a driver to run errands or drive you around in your own car. Use chauffeured transportation for all your shopping trips, parties, airport arrivals and departures.

7. Engage a personal shopper to locate your honeymoon trousseau, lingerie, attendants' gifts, home furnishings.

8. Order one basic beverage—a quality champagne you both enjoy. There will be fewer bar details to see about. Your wine merchant can advise you on quantities.

9. Honeymoon first class. You'll save yourself hassles if you do, since economy flights and accommodations are in greater demand.

10. Fly to a larger city to shop for your dress in a wedding retail establishment if home is a small city or town. A store with a greater volume of business may be able to rush order a dress more effectively to meet your time restrictions, or may have more stock dresses so you can choose one off the rack. Plan two trips—one, to select your gown; the other, to have one-day fittings and alterations.

When Every Penny Counts

1. Telephone ahead to ask basic questions. If the location or service style does not meet your requirements or fall within your budget, do not waste time or tempt yourself by visiting the site.

2. Adjust the time of your ceremony so the reception falls when simpler fare can be served. In midafternoon, for instance, hors d'oeuvres and champagne punch would be sufficient, but at the dinner hour, a meal would be called for.

3. Reduce your flower choices—and the size of your order—by recycling. Let arrangements do double-duty at the ceremony and the reception site. Share ceremony flowers with another bride marrying that day. Select in-season blooms only.

4. Borrow rather than rent. Churches or community centers may have tables, chairs, dishes, flatware.

5. Order only main dishes from a caterer or gourmet food shop. Family members and friends can fill in with salads, breads.

6. Pare down your guest list. Every wedding guest adds to your overall costs and chores—keeping track of invitation responses, thank-you notes; planning table seating, meal service.

7. Examine package deals to see if you really want or need all that is included. You might pare down your photographer's bill if you eliminate your leather album (add one instead to your Wedding Gift Registry list); choose black-and-white photos over color; select a larger number of smaller-sized photographs. Or, create your own album later.

8. Time your wedding to coincide with an upcoming holiday—when the church and reception hall may be decorated anyway; when family members are already planning a get-together.

9. Find out if your department store has a personal shopping service. Because a personal shopper is a store employee, there usually will not be a fee. The shopper can help with locating, choosing, and expediting purchases within the store.

10. Let a family friend host a buffet or picnic meal after your wedding rehearsal. Except for sending thank-you flowers, you two will be relieved of all the planning details for a rehearsal dinner.

Step-by-Step Strategies for Pre-Wedding Parties

Be sure your overloaded calendar can take another entry before you agree to a pre-wedding party. Even events that require no personal attention can add to your schedule in subtle ways—you'll attend a shower, then write thank-you notes, perhaps entertain your future mother-in-law if she's come for the occasion. So think before you say yes: A shower might be even more fun a month *after* your wedding.

Wedding work parties, though, save you time by accomplishing something while everyone's having fun. Therefore do consider champagne- or cake-tasting get-togethers and yard spruce-up parties.

When planning parties, consider the expense of gifts your guests will be giving you. Purchasing an engagement, shower, and wedding gift in an eight-week period may be hard on their budgets.

Pre-wedding parties are the most fun for you and your groom-to-be if planning duties can be shared with others, once you two have made basic decisions.

TIME-SAVING OPTIONS:
Combine work and play. For example, in return for a couple of hours help moving your things to a new apartment, treat your attendants to a picnic supper.

Postpone tasks when possible. Pen a thank-you note now to your bridesmaids and ushers, but shop for your attendants' gifts on your honeymoon. You'll have more time to make them personal.

Keep parties simple. Just take a table at your favorite restaurant and order entrees from the menu. Bring along your own favors for your bridesmaids—perhaps a rose for each one.

BE SURE TO ASK:

Have any relatives or friends offered to host a party?

How long do your clergymember's rehearsals usually last (so you'll know when the rehearsal dinner can be scheduled)?

What time will bridesmaids and ushers be arriving?

DON'T FORGET TO:

_____Record each gift and giver.

_____Arrange transportation and give directions for rehearsal dinner guests.

_____Give thank-you gifts to all child attendants.

_____Inform the wedding party of rehearsal time, plans for rehearsal dinner.

_____Prepare place cards or a seating plan for rehearsal dinner, bridesmaids' luncheon.

_____Propose a toast to parents at rehearsal dinner.

ENGAGEMENT PARTY*

Things to do	Deadline	To be done by	Accomplished (✓)
Visit sites			
Select site			
Reserve site			
Plan guest list			
Purchase invitations			
Address invitations			
Mail invitations			
Hire caterer			
Plan menu			
Discuss meal service			
Arrange for bar service			
Purchase liquor			
Hire bartender			
Hire baker			
Order engagement cake			
Hire florist			
Select flowers and other decorations			
Hire musicians			
Discuss musical selections			

*Usually given by bride's family.

Engagement Party Information

Party site_____

   address_____

   telephone_____

Date and time_____

Hosted by_____

   address_____

   telephone_____

Caterer_____

   address_____

   telephone_____

Bartender_____

   address_____

   telephone_____

Baker_____

   address_____

   telephone_____

Florist_____

   address_____

   telephone_____

Musicians_____

   address_____

   telephone_____

Notes_____

_____

_____

_____

_____

BRIDESMAIDS' LUNCHEON

Things to do	Deadline	To be done by	Accomplished (✓)
Visit sites			
Select site			
Reserve site			
Plan guest list			
Purchase invitations			
Address invitations			
Mail invitations			
Hire caterer or book restaurant			
Plan menu			
Hire baker			
Order bridesmaids' cake			
Hire florist			
Select flowers			
Purchase bridemaids' gifts			
Arrange for engraving			
Purchase favors			
Devise seating plan			
Purchase place cards			
Fill out and distribute			

Bridesmaids' Luncheon Information

Party site_____

    address_____

    telephone_____

Date and time_____

Hosted by_____

    address_____

    telephone_____

Caterer_____

    address_____

    telephone_____

Baker_____

    address_____

    telephone_____

Florist_____

    address_____

    telephone_____

Gifts_____   _____

    _____   _____

    _____   _____

Notes_____

    _____

    _____

    _____

    _____

    _____

BACHELOR PARTY*

Things to do	Deadline	To be done by	Accom-plished (✓)
Visit sites			
Select site			
Reserve site			
Plan guest list			
Purchase invitations			
Address invitations			
Mail invitations			
Hire caterer			
Plan menu			
Discuss meal service			
Arrange for bar service			
Purchase liquor			
Hire bartender			
Plan decorations			
Arrange for transportation			
Book entertainment			
Discuss program selections			

*Usually given by best man and ushers.

Bachelor Party Information

Party site _____

    address _____

    telephone _____

Date and time _____

Hosted by _____

    address _____

    telephone _____

Caterer _____

    address _____

    telephone _____

Liquor store _____

    address _____

    telephone _____

    delivery date and place _____

_____

Bartender _____

    address _____

    telephone _____

Transportation company _____

    address _____

    telephone _____

    size of vehicle _____

    hours hired _____

Entertainment _____

    address _____

continued

telephone _____

fee _____

arrival time _____

Gifts _____

_____

Notes _____

_____

_____

_____

_____

_____

_____

_____

REHEARSAL DINNER*

Things to do	Deadline	To be done by	Accomplished (✓)
Visit sites			
Select site			
Reserve site			
Plan guest list			
Purchase invitations			
Address invitations			
Mail invitations			
Hire caterer			
Plan menu			
Discuss meal service			
Arrange for bar service			
Purchase liquor			
Hire bartender			
Order champagne for toast			
Hire florist			
Select flowers and other decorations			
Devise seating plan			
Purchase place cards			
Fill out and distribute			

*Usually given by groom's family.

Rehearsal Dinner Information

Party site_____

    address_____

    telephone_____

    banquet manager_____

Date and time_____

Hosted by_____

    address_____

    telephone_____

Caterer_____

    address_____

    telephone_____

Liquor store_____

    address_____

    telephone_____

Bartender_____

    address_____

    telephone_____

Florist_____

    address_____

    telephone_____

Notes_____

_____

_____

_____

_____

_____

_____

Step-by-Step Strategies for Wedding Attire

Your wedding clothing either sets the tone or reflects the style of your ceremony and reception. So, when you first visit your bridal or formalwear retailer, you will be asked about the style of your wedding, the time of your ceremony, and the degree of formality you've chosen.

The bride in a hurry must remain flexible. Do understand how the bridal market works before getting your heart set on a particular gown. Bridal magazines introduce the next season's fashions; these gowns will probably not be available for several months. It may be helpful, though, to show a picture to your bridal retailer, who can then suggest a gown with a similar style.

Each store stocks samples of designer dresses for you to try on. Your gown will be custom-made. (That can take from four to six months.) If you are marrying in three months or less, you must concentrate on manufacturers who will respond to a rush; or to those dresses in a manufacturer's line that can be produced quickly, or are sold in varying sizes. Your bridal salesperson should steer you toward the most likely choices and styles. Sometimes you can buy a discontinued sample and have it fitted to your size. No matter how soon you are marrying, you should be able to find a very beautiful, special wedding gown.

Men have an easier time. Men's formalwear is stocked in standard sizes and can be ordered in special sizes, usually within a week. Formalwear dealers, however, prefer to have more time.

Bridesmaids' dresses may be purchased from stock, or ordered from the manufacturer's stock. They can be available in weeks rather than months.

TIME-SAVING OPTIONS:

Bride's attire—

Ask to see "seasonless" dresses (classic designs that remain in the manufacturer's line). The ordering time may be shorter.

Look at discontinued sample dresses on sale.

Order a bridesmaid's dress—in white.

Consider dresses designed for "encore brides," (second-time brides); sometimes these are simpler in design, produced more quickly.

Bridesmaids' attire—

Shop with only one or two bridesmaids to narrow down dress choices. Then bring everyone in—to decide which of the four to six you've selected they would prefer.

Know bridesmaids' sizes and heights when you place the orders. A tall bridesmaid may need extra fabric for her dress length, and that takes more time.

Be prepared to leave a deposit, probably one-third the total amount. Dresses will probably not be ordered from the manufacturer until your order is firm.

Urge bridesmaids to take wedding-day shoes to the fittings, so dresses can be hemmed in proportion to the correct heel height.

Buy wedding jewelry—necklaces, bracelets—as gifts for each bridesmaid. In addition to giving a gift, you'll be assuring a uniform look.

Men's attire—

Obtain measurements from the groomsmen *before* you place the order, so there is no delay in getting the sizes you need.

Place all the menswear orders yourself; it saves

time, consolidates trips to pick up and return, and you'll be assured of a uniform look. Also, you may get your own formalwear free as a thank-you for the large order.

Rent accessories (shoes, neckwear, gloves, vests, cummerbunds, studs, formal shirts) at the same time.

BE SURE TO ASK:

What similar styles are available if your favorite gown is out of your price range?

How many dress features must be altered? Should you look for a simpler design?

How many fittings should you schedule?

Is the manufacturer you've selected reliable with deadlines?

How does the train hook up or veil detach for easy reception movement?

How to describe the gown? Ask for all details—such as name of the lace, type of fabric, style of sleeve and neckline. You'll need this information for your newspaper write-up.

What's the best method for cleaning, storing your dress?

Is the men's formalwear you favor appropriate for the hour, formality of your wedding?

Are the groomsmen's accessories complete?

How may accessories be varied to set the groom and best man apart from the groomsmen?

When must all formalwear be returned?

DON'T FORGET TO:

_____Make a checklist of all the items you'll need when you dress at the wedding site or in a hotel.

_____Bring along nail polish in your wedding-day shade, for last-minute chips and touch-ups. (Bring makeup too.)

_____Take an emergency kit with needle and thread, safety pins, brush and comb, aspirin, tampons, tissues, spare stockings.

_____Bring your bridal shoes. And, scuff the soles and

heels so you don't lose your footing when you step on the aisle runner.

_____Test your eyeglasses at the ceremony site ahead of time. If they darken because of photosensitivity, switch to another pair—or your contacts.

_____Plan ahead for sentimental items—something old, new, borrowed, blue—and a penny in your shoe—if you want to wear them.

_____Arrange with florist for delivery of bouquets and boutonnieres to dressing areas or ceremony site.

Four Tips from Bridal Retailers

1. Be prepared. When you come to a retail shop, have an idea of what you want; know the formality and price range of your bridal ensemble; share your vision of a "dream dress."

2. Keep an open mind. Without giving up your dream, be receptive to a gown with similar styling. Be willing to try on a dress with fewer production details (which makes it easier to get in a hurry).

3. Allow several hours when you look at wedding gowns. You'll need time to try on a variety of dress styles. Bring along your wedding-day shoes (or some with the same height heel), a long-line bra, and other undergarments that will give you the best impression of how the dress looks and fits.

4. Budget your overall time. Look ahead to the next few weeks and plan your movements so you always know what to do next. You'll be able to schedule fittings, shop for bridesmaids' dresses and accessories. Your chores will not seem so stressful with advance planning.

BRIDE'S WEDDING ATTIRE

Things to do	Deadline	To be done by	Accomplished (✓)
Decide on wedding style, formality			
Visit bridal shops			
Select gown (dress)			
Order gown (dress)			
Order headpiece, veil			

Shop for accessories:
 	
    gloves
    purse
    shoes
    stockings
    lingerie
    coat, shawl, or cape
    prayer book
    floral wreath or hat			

Visit florist			
Order bouquet			
Schedule fittings			

Schedule beauty needs:
 	
    hairstyling
    manicure
    makeup			

Bride's Clothing Information

Gown (dress) ordered from_____

    address_____

    telephone_____

    salesperson_____

    promised by_____

    first fitting date_____

Headpiece ordered from_____

    address_____

    telephone_____

    salesperson_____

    promised by_____

Shoes ordered from_____

    address_____

    telephone_____

    promised by_____

Accessories ordered from_____

    salesperson_____

    telephone_____

    promised by_____

Notes_____

_____

_____

_____

_____

_____

_____

_____

_____

BRIDESMAIDS' WEDDING ATTIRE

Things to do	Deadline	To be done by	Accomplished (✓)
Ask bridesmaids to serve			
Ask bridesmaids' sizes, heights			
Visit bridal shops			
Select bridesmaids' gowns (dresses)			
Order gowns (dresses)			
Shop for accessories: headpieces shoes stockings jewelry			
Visit florist			
Order bouquets			
Schedule fittings			
Schedule beauty needs: hairstyling manicure makeup			

Bridesmaids' Clothing Information

Gowns (dresses) ordered from_____

    address_____

    telephone_____

    salesperson_____

    sizes ordered_____

    promised by_____

    first fitting date_____

Headpieces ordered from_____

    address_____

    telephone_____

    salesperson_____

    promised by_____

Shoes ordered from_____

    address_____

    telephone_____

    promised by_____

Accessories ordered from_____

    salesperson_____

    telephone_____

    promised by_____

Notes_____

_____

_____

_____

_____

_____

_____

_____

MEN'S WEDDING ATTIRE

Things to do	Deadline	To be done by	Accom-plished (✓)
Ask ushers to serve			
Request ushers' suit sizes, measurements			
Visit formalwear store			
Decide on style, color			
Reserve menswear			

Shop for accessories:
   shirts
   ties
   cummerbunds
   cuff links, studs
   shoes, socks
   outerwear			

Order boutonnieres			

Men's Clothing Information

Formalwear store _____

    address _____

    telephone _____

    salesperson _____

Number of suits ordered, sizes _____

_____

Fitting dates _____

Delivery _____

Return by _____

Notes _____

_____

_____

_____

_____

_____

_____

_____

Step-by-Step Strategies for the Ceremony

If you are opting for a traditional ceremony (and, even with just thirty days to plan, there is no reason why you can't!), begin by setting priorities. You may have to compromise on some things, but you and your fiancé should decide what's most important to you both.

Next, think about details. You might choose just one or two areas to emphasize, such as selecting interesting music and composing a thoughtful wedding program. Remember: Anticipated details take less time to arrange than last-minute additions. Think ahead. Review each aspect of the ceremony and make lists of what needs to be done.

TIME-SAVING OPTIONS:
Visit sites at the time of day you want to have your ceremony. You'll get the full effect on the first visit without having to return to evaluate lighting and color tone for photography, flowers.

Start a telephone brigade to contact persons on your guest list if your invitations will be mailed later than four weeks before the wedding. Tell everyone to save the date and that invitations will follow.

Hire a calligrapher or social secretary. Have thank-you note envelopes addressed at the same time as the invitations, no matter who is doing the actual writing. It saves looking up addresses on your list twice.

Choose a single instrumentalist, such as a harpist, as your sole ceremony musician. Hire the same person to provide background music at the reception.

Compare the time required to arrange a religious or a civil wedding. If a religious wedding is not important to either of you, you might consider bypassing religious necessities such as counseling or discussion of a previous marriage; ask a judge to officiate.

BE SURE TO ASK:

Are attendants allergic to any flowers? How much could you save by choosing seasonal flowers?

What does the photographer usually wear? How noticeable will his or her movements be? How much lighting is used?

How many passengers will each limousine or car hold?

Are there any music, photography restrictions at ceremony site?

Who should attend the rehearsal?

What are suggested guidelines for clergymember's fees?

What time can deliveries be made to the ceremony site? Who will be there to receive them?

DON'T FORGET TO:

____Proofread invitations carefully; order extra envelopes.

____Provide postage for response envelopes.

____Give photographer list of requests.

____Give band list of requests; ask about overtime fees.

____Plan a place to dress, fix hair and makeup.

____Write out check for best man to give to clergymember after ceremony.

____Bring marriage license.

____Remind best man, maid of honor to bring rings.

_____Bring shoes, headpieces, strapless bras, petti-
coats, gloves, other accessories, emergency kit.

_____Arrange rides for out-of-town guests.

_____Fill wedding cars with gas.

_____Bring telephone numbers for service people.

CEREMONY PLANNING

Things to do	Deadline	To be done by	Accom-plished (✓)
Visit sites			
Select site			
Reserve site			
Meet with clergy or officiant			
Discuss counseling			
Schedule other meetings			
Plan service:			

personal touches
  readings
  greeting
  program
  unity candle
  vows
  hymns			

Arrange for sanctuary furnishings:			

aisle runner
  huppah
  pew markers
  pew tapers
  pew ribbons
  candelabra
  awning, canopy
  red carpet			

Select invitations			
Decide typeface, style			
Type out wording			
Place order			

Things to do	Deadline	To be done by	Accom-plished (✓)
Proofread set type			
Prepare detailed guest list			
Buy stamps, pens			
Arrange for calligrapher or helpers			
Mail invitations			

Order other printing needs:
 	
   announcements
   matchbooks
   cocktail napkins
   programs
   stationery
   thank-you notes			

Arrange for music:
 	
   organist
   instrumentalist
   soloist
   choose hymns and
     other music			

Visit florists			
Research flowers, costs			

Choose:
 	
   pedestal
     arrangements
   altar vases
   potted plants
   entrance
     arrangements
   window arrangements
   pew, pillar treatments			

Visit photographers' studios			

Things to do	Deadline	To be done by	Accomplished (✓)
Research photography costs (compare costs for package deals)			
Arrange for portrait			
Prepare shot list			
Book photographer, videographer			
Sign contracts			
Decide on photographic style			
Determine lighting, electrical needs			
Book wedding cars or limousines			
Arrange rides for out-of-town guests			
Plan for a getaway car or limousine			
Prepare gratuities for: clergy organist sexton altarboys			
Schedule rehearsal			
Remind all participants of date, time			
Meet legal requirements: get blood tests apply for marriage license			

Ceremony Site Information

Name of site_____

    address_____

    telephone_____

    contact person_____

Officiant_____

    address_____

    telephone_____

    contact person_____

Equipment to be supplied_____

_____

_____

Date, time of rehearsal_____

Notes_____

_____

_____

_____

_____

_____

_____

_____

_____

_____

_____

_____

_____

_____

Stationer Information

Name of firm_____

   address_____

   telephone_____

   contact person_____

Contents of order_____

Contract signed (yes)_____ (no)_____

Date promised for proofreading_____

Date of delivery_____

Delivery arrangements_____

Organized by_____

   telephone_____

Cost_____

Notes_____

_____

_____

_____

_____

_____

_____

_____

_____

_____

_____

_____

_____

Ceremony Musicians Information

Name of organist, musicians_____

_____

   address(es)_____

   telephone(s)_____

   contact person_____

Contract signed (yes)_____ (no)_____

Processional music_____

_____

Recessional music_____

_____

Name of soloist(s)_____

   telephone(s)_____

   vocal selections_____

_____

Fees_____

Arrival time_____

Organized by_____

   telephone_____

Notes_____

_____

_____

_____

_____

_____

_____

Transportation Information

Name of firm_____

   address_____

   telephone_____

   contact person_____

Contract signed (yes)_____ (no)_____

Number of vehicles_____

Arrival time_____

Rental fee per hour_____

Driver_____

   passengers_____

_____

_____

Driver_____

   passengers_____

_____

_____

Driver_____

   passengers_____

_____

_____

Notes_____

_____

_____

_____

_____

Step-by-Step Strategies for the Reception

Planning your wedding reception will call upon your best organizational and party-giving skills. First get the big picture in place—the site, the menu, the logistics. Then picture the party in progress and fill in the details. What's missing from the table? Where's the receiving line? What's a great backdrop for photographs? Who's keeping the party running smoothly? *Anticipating* is the key to good party planning.

TIME-SAVING OPTIONS:
Engage a music consultant to research sounds, songs, local talent.

Hire a party planner to guide you in the use of space for your home wedding. A fresh eye can create surprises in your own familiar environment.

Assign a site consultant the job of searching for a unique reception site.

Choose a restaurant reception site and be assured of the stylish ambiance already provided—tablecloths, table flowers, china and glassware, as well as a tasty array of food (for a small group, order individually, from the standard menu) and practiced service by the waiters.

Fashion a wedding cake quickly by stacking two bakery-purchased iced layer cakes of varying diameters (perhaps a six-inch cake atop a ten-inch one). Then decorate beautifully with fresh flowers.

BE SURE TO ASK:

Is the reception site to be shared with another wedding group? How are facilities divided? How is privacy insured?

Where's the best place to set up the receiving line?

What are the reception site/band/caterer cancellation fees? What are the overtime charges? When do they begin?

What dance music appeals to all age groups? How many dancers will the dance floor hold?

How many drinks does each bottle of liquor provide?

How many glasses are poured per bottle of champagne? Is there an opening fee per bottle?

When will the cake be delivered? Will it be assembled and decorated before guests arrive? Is the cake cut by banquet staff?

DON'T FORGET TO:

_____Plan for foul weather (valet parking so guests can enter the reception site quickly; a tent for an outdoor reception).

_____Write out photographer's shot list.

_____Assign photographer's helper to round up guests.

_____Ask someone to take charge of the guest book and be sure there are plenty of pens so everyone can sign.

_____Plan for dancing. How will you hold or fasten your train? What will you do with your headpiece or veil? How will you arrange your hair after removing the headpiece?

_____Bring seating chart, distribute place cards.

_____Arrange for someone to watch gifts, transport them home.

_____Honor someone by asking him to say a blessing over the bread, or grace for the reception meal.

_____Have going-away clothes delivered to the reception site.

_____Assign someone the job of returning tuxedoes, taking your gown home.

_____Check if you must include photographer, musicians in the guest count for meals.

WEDDING RECEPTION

Things to do	Deadline	To be done by	Accomplished (✓)
Research reception sites			
Telephone with questions			
Visit good prospects			
Reserve site with deposit, contract			
Arrange for hospitality room			
Discuss table arrangement, linens, decorations			
Arrange for coat check			
Arrange for valet parking			
Arrange for gift table, security			
Arrange for restroom attendant, guest towels, soap			
Deliver seating chart, place cards, favors			
Deliver guest book, pens			
Research caterers			
Plan menu			
Consider family recipes, ethnic traditions			
Discuss food service with caterer or banquet manager			

Things to do	Deadline	To be done by	Accomplished (✓)
Hire waiters and waitresses			
Give caterer final guest count for meals, specify special diet plates (kosher, low-salt, vegetarian)			
Research bakers			
Sample, select flavors, decorations			
Order wedding cake			
Order groom's cake (boxes if needed)			
Select cake topper			
Purchase or borrow cake knife			
Research liquor stores			
Order liquor, champagne, after-dinner cordials, other beverages			
Hire bartender			
Research florists			
Choose colors, flowers			
Order arrangements for: head table guest tables cake table room decoration			

Things to do	Deadline	To be done by	Accomplished (✓)
Research bands			
Audition good prospects			
Book, sign contract with band			
Hire soloists			
Hire entertainment			
Give band leader song list, timetable, order of first dance			
Discuss master of ceremonies role, ask band leader to serve			
Research rental equipment			
Rent needed furnishings:			
tables			
chairs			
china			
flatware			
glassware			
serving platters, bowls			
linens			
sound equipment			
tent			
dance floor			
Arrange deliveries, pick-ups			
Plan reception timetable (see chart pp. 96–97)			

Things to do	Deadline	To be done by	Accom-plished (✓)
Arrange for gratuities for: 　maître d'hôtel or 　　banquet manager 　musicians 　chef 　waiters, waitresses 　bartenders 　restroom attendants 　coat check attendants 　valet parking staff 　limousine drivers 　security guard			

PLANNING YOUR RECEPTION TIMETABLE

A smooth-running party—especially your wedding celebration—will seem effortless with careful advance planning. Choose the activities you'll be including from the list below, and decide when to start and end each segment.

Event	Time allotted
Wedding party, guests arrive at reception site	
Photographer begins shots of wedding party, families	
Wedding party, families form receiving line	
Guests pick up table-seating cards	
Waiters, waitresses serve drinks, champagne, hors d'oeuvres	
Master of ceremonies announces dinner, buffet (for dinner, specify each course)	
Honored person offers blessing, grace	
Best man proposes toast, others follow	
Bride and groom begin traditional "first dance," wedding party and guests join in	
Waiters, waitresses clear tables	
Master of ceremonies announces cake-cutting ceremony	

Event	Time allotted
Families introduce ethnic dances, good-luck rituals	
Bride throws bouquet	
Groom throws garter	
Bride and groom change into traveling clothes	
Bride and groom say good-bye to families	
Bride and groom depart for honeymoon	
Host and hostess say good-bye to guests	

Reception Site Information

Party site _____

  address _____

  telephone _____

  contact person _____

Contract signed (yes) _____ (no) _____

Date and time _____

Organized by _____

  telephone _____

Notes _____

_____

_____

_____

_____

_____

_____

_____

_____

_____

_____

_____

_____

_____

_____

_____

_____

_____

_____

Florist Information

Florist_____

    address_____

    telephone_____

    contact person_____

Delivery time_____

Contract signed (yes)_____ (no)_____

Floral selections_____

Notes_____

_____

_____

_____

_____

_____

_____

_____

_____

_____

_____

_____

_____

_____

_____

_____

_____

_____

_____

_____

Catering Information

Caterer_____

    address_____

    telephone_____

    contact person_____

Arrival time_____

Names of waiters/waitresses_____

Name of bartender_____

Attire requested_____

Organized by_____

    telephone_____

Contract signed (yes)_____ (no)_____

Time party ends_____

Number of guests to be served_____

Menu_____

_____

_____

_____

Notes_____

_____

_____

_____

_____

_____

_____

_____

Photography/Videography Information

Photography studio _____

    photographer _____

    assistant _____

    address _____

    telephone _____

Contract signed (yes) _____ (no) _____

Arrival time _____

Attire _____

Hours _____

Cost _____

Albums _____

Delivery date _____

Shots contact person _____

    telephone _____

Notes _____

_____

_____

_____

_____

_____

_____

_____

_____

_____

_____

_____

_____

Music Information

Musicians_____

    address_____

    telephone_____

    contact person_____

Contract signed (yes)_____ (no)_____

Arrival time_____

Playing time/breaks_____

Attire_____

Payment required_____

Organized by_____

    telephone_____

Notes_____

_____

_____

_____

_____

_____

_____

_____

_____

_____

_____

_____

_____

_____

_____

Cake Information

Baker_____

    address_____

    telephone_____

    contact person_____

Contract signed (yes)_____ (no)_____

Delivery time_____

Payment required_____

Colors/description/filling_____

_____

Cake topper_____

Notes_____

_____

_____

_____

_____

_____

_____

_____

_____

_____

_____

_____

_____

_____

_____

_____

Step-by-Step Strategies for the Honeymoon

Even if it's just overnight or for a weekend, treat yourselves to a private, pampered beginning to married life. That special time together can help you shift gears after all the busy preparations of the preceding weeks and get you back in touch with essential things about each other. Decide what you can spend, how much time to allow, and what type of vacation would be pleasurable for both of you.

TIME-SAVING OPTIONS:
Use a travel agent.

Plan a weekend away now; honeymoon later.

Make it a vacation wedding for you, your families, close friends. Large resort hotels often have wedding coordinators to help with local needs.

Call resorts directly; take advantage of last-minute cancellations.

Book a luxury "package" such as a cruise, a tour.

Choose an out-of-season or "off-peak" place. Arrangements will be easier.

BE SURE TO ASK:
What's the weather like at your honeymoon site?

How much luggage are you allowed?

Do you need immunization?

What's the airline overbooking policy? How soon should you arrive at the airport?

How far from the airport is your hotel?

Where can you pick up/return a rental car?

What are the best restaurants at your honeymoon location? Are reservations necessary?

Where can you obtain tourist information once you're there?

DON'T FORGET TO:

——Pack birth-control items/medications/contact lens equipment/tickets/passports in carry-on luggage.

——Load luggage in getaway car.

——Buy film, bring camera.

——Write down guidebook recommendations.

——Take along traveler's checks (both of you, in case of an emergency); keep list of check numbers in a separate place.

——Carry travel agent's telephone number, hotel address and directions in your handbag.

——Bring along going-away clothes for changing at the reception site.

——Pack address book/telephone credit card/converted currency in your handbag.

HONEYMOON

Things to do	Deadline	To be done by	Accom-plished (√)
Visit travel agents			
Visit library			
Read travel ads, magazines, guidebooks			
Book transportation			
Book lodgings			
Arrange day trips			
Rent car			
Renew/apply for passports, visas			
Purchase traveler's checks, sign immediately			
Convert currency			
Obtain immunizations			
Obtain travel medications			
Shop for trousseau needs:			
His			
Hers			
Arrange departure transportation			
Confirm travel plans			

Honeymoon Information

Destination _____

    address _____

    telephone _____

    contact person _____

Airline _____

    departure (time, flight #) _____

    return (time, flight #) _____

Travel agent _____

    address _____

    telephone _____

Cost _____

    form of payment _____

    date of payment _____

Itinerary _____

_____

_____

_____

_____

_____

Notes _____

_____

_____

_____

_____

_____

_____

_____

Hints for a Healthy Wedding-Day Glow

With so many demands on your time, brief day-by-day health and beauty routines are easiest, and pamper the spirit as well as the body.

Five Do's

1. Stick to a balanced, nutritious diet, even if you're trying to lose weight. On wedding day, if you're too excited to eat, avoid lightheadedness with small, nutritious snacks.
2. To keep your hands attractive, wear protective gloves when you do heavy work or use strong cleaning solutions. Learn to use nail tips—great for emergency manicure repairs.
3. If you'll be using birth-control pills, start a couple of months before your wedding (three is optimal) so your body will have time to adjust.
4. Do break in your new shoes (both of you!) so your wedding day is not spoiled by blisters and sore feet.
5. Watch caffeine and alcohol intake and get enough sleep—they're the best remedies for jitters.

Five Don'ts

1. Don't try for a sudden tan—either outdoors or in a tanning booth. You may end up with peeling blis-

ters accessorizing your lovely wedding gown. Instead, protect your skin with sunscreen and moisturizer.

2. If your groom wants to shave off a beard or mustache, be sure there's time for that pale sensitive skin underneath to adjust to shaving irritations and get some color back.

3. Don't switch from glasses to contact lenses if there isn't time to break them in. (Check with your eye doctor.) Red, teary eyes will interfere with your good time.

4. Don't get your ears pierced unless you have a couple of months to get used to them, clear up any inflammations, and graduate from studs to pretty earrings.

5. Don't do anything rash to your face or hair—changing makeup or hair color, using a new facial mask, experimenting with a permanent. You want to look like *you* on your wedding day!

Workable Weddings: Unique Solutions to Common Problems

If hastening your wedding plans has created some problems, there are all kinds of nontraditional yet wonderful wedding solutions that may meet the needs of your situation.

Problem: You can't agree on a religious service. Your groom-to-be is a Buddhist. Your Roman Catholic relatives are uncomfortable about an interfaith ceremony. There isn't time for educating families or devising a service that blends traditions. What are your options?

Solution: civil ceremony. A civic official, such as a judge or mayor, may perform your ceremony at any location within his or her jurisdiction, in compliance with state and local laws. Check out this alternative. Civil ceremonies can be arranged quickly, depending on the official's schedule.

Solution: marriage blessing. Following a legal ceremony, your union receives the sanction of one (or both) churches in a short liturgy of prayer and affirmation at each house of worship. It may be private (no witnesses required) or witnessed by a large gathering.

Problem: Your families are too distant, and time is too short for conventional wedding plans. When a job transfer precipitates hasty wedding arrangements, your families may have trouble making travel and lodging arrangements. How can you make it easier for them, yet still marry quickly?

Solution: conference-call wedding. If you make arrangements ahead of time with the telephone company, a three-way call would let both families listen in to a wedding ceremony held in your own city, while they gather in their individual hometowns. A speakerphone will amplify your vows. Celebrate with reception parties when you next visit home.

Solution: wedding trip. Plan a honeymoon/wedding trip for yourselves, and invite any family member who can to come along (at their own expense). The date and the setting are your decisions. You might take a quick head count and reserve a block of rooms, but let individual participants complete their own arrangements.

Solution: reaffirmation. Why not have a simple "official" wedding with local friends and relatives, then plan a reaffirmation, which can take the same form as a wedding ceremony, sometime in the future. Certain phrases, such as "do you acknowledge" are substituted for "do you take," since you are already married.

Problem: You want a reunion, not just a wedding. Chances are, if you've been busy with romance, you haven't had enough time to keep up with old and far-flung friends. You've organized this magnificent event to bring them all together—but can't bear to have the fun end so soon.

Solution: weekend wedding. Use your imagination to create a full schedule of activities (baseball game, bus tour, slide show) and get-togethers (barbecue, brunch, pool party) around the main event— matrimony. Guests traveling a distance will appreciate jitney or car pool service to get around. Do added activities necessarily mean lots more work for you? You might actually have an easier time because relatives and neighbors may offer to organize or host an entire function. You two needn't stay long at all events.

Problem: Your sister planned her wedding first. Her wedding is just six weeks away, but you two have discovered your dream house and are determined to marry *before* you buy it. Can relatives be expected to travel to two weddings in such a short space of time?

> *Solution: double wedding.* If your sister is willing, a double wedding can be a loving family experience. Since her plans are already in place, you two might split expenses and share all the last-minute details. Usually for double weddings the two couples would decide on a mutually acceptable style, but in this case, your clothing should conform to your sister's choices.

Problem: You want a small private ceremony . . . now! Both married before, you and your fiancé are anxious to tie the knot and blend your two sets of children into a new family as quickly as possible. You want a ceremony with little fanfare—just families present to share the private moment of commitment. But, you want to celebrate with friends too! How to have it both ways?

> *Solution: rectory wedding.* A clergymember will marry you in his or her study, or in a private chapel, with just two witnesses (these must be of legal age) or a few family members in attendance. Then, invite guests to join in the revelry immediately afterward, or at a party planned in the near future.

> *Solution: elopement.* The two of you (kids, too, if you have them) might slip away to a state, such as California, where there is no wait for a license and none after obtaining it (the latter a legal requirement in some states). A justice of the peace or civic official can do the honors. Then, when you return, you newlyweds can throw a joyous announcement party.

Speedy Solutions to Wedding Crises

You've dreamed of a very special wedding ring, but time doesn't permit having one custom designed. Should you use a family ring? Would it be unlucky?

Traditionally, Jewish brides are married with plain gold bands, unbroken by design or stones (to symbolize an honest contract). However, many wear a more ornate ring later. You two might exchange simple gold bands (or family rings) during your ceremony; then, perhaps for your first anniversary, create that ring you've envisoned. You can, if you wish, ask your minister to bless the new ring with a special prayer.

You've just discovered your reception site double-booked by mistake. Luckily, you find a new party place, but how to let everyone know?

Even with rush printing, there's not enough time to mail a notice. Get together a telephone relay team and divide up the guest list among them. Send a mailgram to any guests you cannot reach by phone. A slightly different system may be used to keep your wedding party abreast of late-breaking developments: It's called a telephone tree. You call your maid of honor to relay any news, she calls a bridesmaid, who passes it along to her assigned call. The last in line always phones you back and repeats the message, so you know your news has gotten through.

Because of a sudden job opportunity in Europe, your wedding is being held three months earlier than you'd planned. You don't want to store or ship wedding presents. How can you tactfully let people know you'd rather receive gifts of money?

It's not considered good form to state this directly. But your parents and bridesmaids will have many opportunities to let others know your preference. And, if someone asks you directly, by all means be honest. Despite your best efforts, however, you should know that some people may still prefer to purchase a gift.

It seemed best to have a small church wedding in the city where you both work, then visit both your faraway families. But without your father to escort you and the groom's brother to be best man, you're having trouble filling traditional roles. What are your alternatives?

It's not necessary for anyone to escort you down the aisle. Some couples do this: The bride walks halfway down alone, then her groom joins her and they walk the rest of the way together. You can also cross gender lines with your choice of attendants. Your groom may ask a female friend to be best woman, you might choose a man of honor. Or, have "groom's people," several close friends who help seat guests, pass out programs or hymnals.

You started out being very careful about wedding planning decisions, but as the date draws closer, you feel you're making too many snap judgments. Now you're looking for an apartment. Though you haven't found anything just right, you're ready to settle on one. How else will you ever get moved in on time?

When time is scarce, why not postpone some non-essentials until after the wedding? Is it really necessary to return from your honeymoon to a completely settled apartment? Why not put off combining your living quarters until later, stay in a motel for a week or two, return to a parent's home, or live in your small apartment a while longer? Do some talking on your honeymoon about your future housing, lifestyle, and budget.

You've purchased the bridesmaids' dresses, but for three of the four who live out of town, there will be little time for fittings. Should you take a chance and have a dress mailed to each bridesmaid for altering?

Get careful measurements from distant bridesmaids and ushers before you order. List exact height, dress size (bridesmaids); inseam, collar, and jacket size (ushers). Perhaps you could hire a seamstress to be on hand the day before your wedding to alter all the dresses. It may take too long to find one style suited to different sized bridesmaids, so why not let each shop for a dress she likes within your color and formality scheme. Also, if you limit the size of your wedding party, arrangements will be simpler.

You've just learned that your aunt and uncle are visiting this country from their native South America in January. Your wedding is planned for June. The family is pressing you to hold the wedding earlier so the visiting relatives can attend. Should you move your wedding date up? Can you plan everything so fast?

Call a wedding consultant. These wedding magicians are in business to handle every aspect of your wedding. You will still set the style and budget, and make all other major decisions. But the legwork— scouting sites, services—will be handled with care and expertise by your professional planner. You'll be presented with feasible options within your budget. Also, rushed wedding plans go more smoothly in January than in June, since fewer weddings take place then and everything from reception sites to florists is more available.

Your mother will be heartbroken if you do not wear the wedding dress that has already been worn by five brides in the family. You take the family tradition seriously, but nevertheless want to feel special. How?

Every bride wants to feel unique on her wedding day. If you must wear a borrowed dress, whether contemporary or antique, two things will help make it "yours." Have it altered so it fits you impeccably (you may have to promise the lender to restore it to its original size). And, take the dress to your bridal retailer to find just the right headpiece, gloves, accessories to give your ensemble a distinctive look.

You're looking forward to marrying in your hometown, but dread the confusion and crowding at your parents' home that's bound to accompany all the returning siblings and their families. How can you arrange for some privacy for yourself without hurting anyone's feelings?

You might visit with your parents at home a day or two ahead of the wedding, then book yourself into a hotel the day before so you can insure some last-minute privacy and enjoy the luxury of maid and room service—and a bathroom to yourself! Do pack carefully so you have everything you need.

If you want to stay at your old homestead, find ways to accommodate other family members nearby. Look to the neighbors—would anyone lend a spare room? Or, rent or borrow a recreational vehicle, trailer home, or camper to park in your driveway. Then, overflow family can be near, while you two can stay at your homes without too much chaos.

Your photographer took rolls and rolls of pictures at your wedding reception. But, since you forgot to make a list of "special shots," he managed to miss your groom dancing with his grandmother and a shot of you two toasting with your heirloom goblets. What can you do now?

You can never recapture that day, but you might organize another photo opportunity so that candids can be taken of you with those special people. Why not host a "come-as-you-were" party at your new apartment? You could wear your gown; your groom, a tux; his grandmother, her special dress. Serve champagne and help others recreate the wedding day mood by showing all the slides, movies, videotapes, photographs you've collected so far. Then, have the photographer on hand to snap those missing shots or pictures of this new gathering to add to your album.

Your wedding is only one month away and you're getting panicky about all that's left to do. Even so, you're uneasy about asking friends at work to help out. Your supervisor might think your wedding planning is diminishing your job performance. Would it be a mistake to involve colleagues at work?

It can look unprofessional. And, you might then feel obligated to invite someone who helped you with wedding errands, even though your guest list is getting too large already. It's best to make it clear from the beginning that you'll talk about wedding plans on private time—your coffee break, lunch hour, after work. Office friends can be helpful in the same ways they would be at other hectic times—picking up a sandwich for you at lunch so you can devote your whole hour to telephone calls; scheduling a project a week early so your honeymoon vacation plans will work. Do let colleagues know you'll appreciate contacts, tips, but will follow up on them yourself. You might hire an office secretary to "moonlight" as your wedding assistant at your home in the evening, but don't expect anyone to be happy to help out gratis.

Changing Your Mind

Fast-paced wedding arrangements may create intense stress. Don't rush blindly ahead if serious conflict develops. Decide if you are experiencing pre-wedding "jitters," or are having valid second thoughts.

"Jitters" are normal anxiety—physical or emotional—that come from adding stress to your routine and anticipating both the pleasure and tension of your wedding day. *Remember,* "jitters" are frayed nerves, *not* paralyzing apprehensions.

True distress signals, though, may have less to do with normal anticipatory anxiety and more with readiness to make this final commitment. Call for time out if serious problems emerge—blocked communication, family feuds, sexual incompatibility. Then, consider these alternatives:

· Talk to each other openly about your conflicts.
· Discuss your worries with your clergymember.
· Meet with a couple counselor.

If, after honest effort at working things out, you decide the wedding must be cancelled, act quickly. The standard method of cancellation is to issue printed cards in a style similar to the wedding invitation. You'll need time to get them made up, addressed, and delivered. Even for a rush order, your stationer will probably need forty-eight hours. You may also send handwritten notes, telegrams, or mail-grams. Faster still: Organize friends, relatives, to divide up the guest list and inform everyone by telephone of the change. No explanation is necessary.

Your Wedding Day

The planning's done . . . your wedding garments are pressed and ready . . . the guests are assembling . . . and now your moment is at hand.

So—let go of lists, duties, and all thoughts of things you've forgotten. Though you had to hurry beforehand, this is the time to slow down and enjoy the fruits of your efforts. Take a moment to breathe deeply and relax.

Your careful planning, well thought-out decisions, and cooperative efforts have enabled you to put together a magnificent wedding celebration. Congratulate yourself for accomplishing so much in such a short space of time.

Competent, composed, beautiful . . . here comes the bride!

Notes

Notes

Notes

Notes

Index